Mary C

BRAVE FAITH

A 31 Day Devotional Journey

MARY GEISEN

Mary Geisen

DEDICATED TO:

My Dad

You showed me what it looked like to live an authentic life, always staying true to your values and who God created you to be. Your courageous journey the last six months of your life illustrated brave faith and showed me firsthand what it looked like. You modeled acceptance and understanding throughout your life. You taught me how to listen to others as if no one else was in the room. You loved your family well and cared for everyone. You are the bravest man I know and you will always be my hero.

My sons Nicholas and Daniel

Your ability to dream and hope for the future spurs me on to do the same.
Your faith in God reflects who you are and how you live your lives.
Your walk forward in brave faith shows me how I can be brave too.
Thank you for teaching me and walking ahead of me in your faith journeys so I can find my way.

Mary Geisen

Mary Geisen

CONTENTS

ACKNOWLEDGMENTS

I would like to acknowledge the help of...
The following friends who so graciously contributed their words to this devotional.

Holly Solomon Barrett – www.hollybarrett.org

LeeAnn Taylor – www.leeanngtaylor.com

Jen Daugherty -
https://faithmustardseed.wordpress.com

Marcy Hanson – www.marcynellhanson.com

A big thank you to the beautiful ladies in my Mastermind group, Debbie, Holly and Patti, who kept me motivated, encouraged and somewhat sane throughout the process of creating this book.

Finally, a shout out goes to my son, Daniel and his wife, Kayla who were my second and third set of eyes as we looked for mistakes or formatting glitches.
Keep in mind that "to err is human, to forgive, divine"!
☺ Alexander Pope

Introduction- What is Brave?

If hearing the word "brave" sends your stomach into a tizzy or causes your palms to sweat profusely, this book is for you. If you believe other people are brave, but would never use that word to describe yourself, this book is for you. If brave is a concept that seems unattainable, this book is for you.

Together we will journey to brave faith. We will take baby steps and explore questions such as:

Does brave mean we need to step out of our comfort zone?
How do we become brave?
How do we face our fears and overcome them?
Can we be brave when we are asked to stay right where we are?
Can we become brave on our own?
Will God lead us to brave faith if we say "yes" to Him?

I spent 31 days last October exploring brave and writing about it each day. I read about brave, explored what it means in my own life and the path needed to journey to brave faith. The biggest lesson I learned is that brave is ongoing and continues to evolve and mature while we become braver one step at a time.

You will find 31 days of devotionals exploring brave faith to help you go deeper and understand what brave looks like in your own life. Verses are suggested each day for reflection as well as a "Take Five" section with questions and ideas to dig deeper into your brave journey.

I am praying for you as you begin this brave journey. I want to assure you that you are not alone on this path. I am still walking toward brave faith myself as God opens my eyes to a deeper understanding.

My prayer and hope for you is to gain a deeper understanding of who you are and what brave looks like in your life.

You are loved. You are unique. You are an amazing child of God. Most of all, **YOU** are brave!

A JOURNEY TO BRAVE FAITH
Day 1

Brave is a journey. A step by step walk, moving forward, leaving fear, uncertainty and other stumbling blocks behind. It is reminding yourself that as a child of God, you were made for more.

As a middle-aged woman, my days of being daring seem to be slowly waning. I look at my sons and those younger than myself and see a confidence and ability to dream as well as take chances that I seem to have lost. I question whether "brave" is only for the younger generation or if I can find brave too?

I am learning that brave is for everyone. The times when we would never describe ourselves as brave, are the times God is working on the inside by boldly building up who we believe we are. He is taking our deepest insecurities and making them new again.

We don't need to look far in the Bible to find brave characters. Each person God called, from Abraham to Paul, suffered from believing they were not brave enough until they left their doubts behind and let God make them new again.

Joshua is one of those characters who tells a story of faith, courage and obedience. God prepared the Israelites for 40 years as they wandered the desert. They questioned God over and over and doubted God's promise but eventually made their way into Canaan-the Promised Land. God prepared Joshua and the Israelites by teaching them the importance of courageous and consistent faith. Brave faith requires courage and consistency. It is a journey of constantly letting go of whatever is holding us back and letting God lead us into the Promised Land.

God reminds us of a beautiful truth in these words from Joshua.

Have I not commanded you? Be strong and courageous. Do not be afraid; do not be discouraged, for the Lord your God will be with you wherever you go.
Joshua 1:9

You might believe that being brave is for the Abrahams and Joshuas of this world. However, God is calling each of us to bravely walk with Him. He believes in us enough to call us His child.

Verses for Reflection:

Genesis 22
Joshua 1: 6-9
Acts 9

Take Five:
(Five minutes to reflect, journal or sit and be with God)

1. Chapter 22 in Genesis tells the story of God asking Abraham to sacrifice his son, Isaac. How does this story begin to teach us about brave faith?

2. Based on the promise in Joshua 1:9, how does knowing God will be with us wherever we go help you as you begin this journey to brave faith?

3. In Acts 9, Paul is commissioned by Jesus to go forth and spread the Good News to the Gentiles. How does God call you in your life to serve Him?

WHAT IS BRAVE?
Day 2

What is brave? Oh, if I only knew the answer to that question! I am thinking I can tell you what brave is not, but then I stop myself because brave looks different for everyone. My brave is not going to look like your brave and that is okay.

When we step out of our comfort zone, we are brave. I always tell people that my comfort zone is very small, so brave steps often happen when I choose to become uncomfortable. How about you? What does your brave look like?

In the book, "*Let's All Be Brave*" by Annie Downs, every page is full of real life moments that teach us that brave does not have to be extraordinary, but in fact can be very ordinary. Annie calls us to action right from the very start and asks us to take the leap that scares us to death. Bold words for someone like me, who is naturally not brave. Her words teach us that brave is not clear cut and it is full of rules.

She says...

There is no formula and there are no rules. There is the Bible, our guidebook for all things, but other than that, being brave is organic and spiritual and a unique journey for each person.

So when we try to assign specific words to describe "brave" we are going to find that we actually just need to start the journey to find out what brave is for us.

Brave steps happen when we choose to be uncomfortable.

Let's walk this journey together and find out what brave faith looks like. Let's turn to God's truth to speak into our hearts and teach us what steps are needed to move forward out of our own comfort zones. *Let's all be brave!*

Verses for Reflection:

2 Timothy 1:7
Philippians 4:13
Jeremiah 29:11-14

Take Five:
(Five minutes to reflect, journal or sit and be with God)

1. Annie Downs writes that being brave is "a unique journey." What does your brave journey look like and how do you turn to God's Word to guide you?

2. If you were to describe the size of your comfort zone, what would you say? How will you begin to grow your comfort zone to include brave faith?

3. 2 Timothy 1:7 (NLT) says: *"For God has not given us a spirit of fear and timidity, but of power, love, and self-discipline."* How will this truth help you as you move forward in brave faith?

BRAVE IS SHOWING UP
Day 3

I am an introvert. I love sitting in coffee shops by myself, engaging in one on one conversations with a friend and walking in my favorite park. My personality screams small, intimate, quiet and avoid crowds at all costs. I ask myself often if "brave" is something that describes who I am especially after sharing this peek into my personality.

I am in awe of those people who seem to jump into new experiences without any hesitation. I am a "stand on the edge looking in" kind of girl and this has always worked well for me. It's not that I never jump in, but I need to think it through and process the possibilities first.

God shows us that brave faith does not require giant steps, but multiple baby steps to keep us moving forward. Many days this looks like just showing up even when your introverted self would rather stay home.

When we are called to show up, God promises to show up right alongside us. Walking into a room full of people whom we do not know is brave for someone like me, but as many times as I have ventured into a new situation, I have been surprised an equal amount of times by how smoothly it went.

Brave faith is walking one step forward and just showing up, especially on those days we do not feel like it. God will meet us in the space of doubt and courage and make it work for His good.

Verses for Reflection:

Psalm 16:11
1 Timothy 6:12
Psalm 139:7-8

Take Five:
(Five minutes to reflect, journal or sit and be with God)

1. Imagine just showing up and embracing a new situation. Write down all of the feelings this brings about in your journal.

2. The verses for reflection today revolve around the theme of presence. Choose one of the verses to reflect on further.

3. There are times we are called to just show up. What will help you take the step forward when that happens?

Mary Geisen

KEEP BECOMING
Day 4

    Along the way to brave faith, there is a process of evolving, the chance to unfold into who God has always planned we would be. If we were already brave, we wouldn't need this devotional or dare I say we wouldn't need God. But we are imperfect people who strive for perfection and the only way to reach that goal is to step out with God into the unknown that God makes known. Preston Yancey writes very simply that Jesus isn't going to call the already brave. His words were an eye opener to the possibilities of how our progress is contingent on choosing to move forward into becoming.

Mr. Yancey writes:

> **Jesus doesn't ask the already brave to do brave things. Jesus asks the becoming brave to keep becoming.**

    Today we have the chance to become the person God has written about in our stories. We can choose to be known as a child of God and step out bravely as God calls us. Our imperfections will threaten to intercept the pieces of courage we are learning, but God's story is already written. Let's allow God's perfect story for us to be read in full as we become more like Him.

Imperfect people who strive to be perfect step out with God into the unknown that He makes known.

Verses for Reflection:

Psalm 139:16
Psalm 27:1
Philippians 2:7-8

Take Five:
(Five minutes to reflect, journal or sit and be with God)

1. How will you move forward into becoming "you" today?

2. Now that you know God does not choose the already brave, how does this help you to know you can attain brave faith?

3. We each have a unique story written by God. In order to move forward on this journey to brave faith, we need to allow the story to unfold as God has written it. How will you seek your own journey to becoming you?

Brave is taking one step closer to living a life in which God is in charge.

Passage Through Grace

BECOMING BRAVE
Day 5

I never believed the word **"brave"** is one others would choose to describe me, but sometimes what we believe about ourselves is not what God has chosen for us. This journey I am walking right now is all about brave and it does not always look brave from the outside, but the work going on inside is huge and it's creating a brave space.

Becoming brave is a process of forward, backward and even sideways. It is stretching who I am to become who God wants me to be. It is a constant struggle between stepping toward brave while at the same time turning away in fear. My steps look very much like the ones Peter took when he walked on the water toward Jesus, one dark and stormy night. Peter took that leap of faith, but several seconds later, he froze with fear when He took His eyes off Jesus. *Isn't that how most of us react when we try to remain faithful: as soon as something draws us away, we sink?*

We are only brave when we keep our eyes focused on God. Each step toward God leads us on the journey of embracing brave faith. It is knowing that sometimes being brave requires faith of the unknown while at the same time knowing that God makes all things known as

He is ready. Brave is taking one step closer to living a life in which God is in charge.

I recently began reading John Ortberg's book, *If You Want to Walk on Water You've Got to Get Out of the Boat*. Wow! It only took reading the preface to know that this book will preach. Mr. Ortberg asks us to take a walk and begins to share how you must become a water walker if you want to experience a deeper presence with God.

We are all made for this even though in our hearts we might not believe it. Mr. Ortberg describes the patterns we find in Scripture when God calls us to more. He shares the following five patterns:

1. There is always a call.

2. There is always fear.

3. There is always reassurance.

4. There is always a decision.

5. There is always a changed life.

Saying "yes" to brave faith will be the hardest and scariest thing we do, but it is the best way to learn who God has chosen us to be. We become brave in our yeses and noes but it is always because we have turned to God to lead the way.

Verses for Reflection:

Matthew 14:27-29
Deuteronomy 28:9-11
Isaiah 11: 3-4

Take Five:
(Five minutes to reflect, journal or sit and be with God)

1. Reread the list of five patterns we find in Scripture from John Ortberg. Which one is the biggest challenge for you to embrace in your brave journey?

2. Based on your answer above, give yourself some time to reflect on why you chose the answer you did.

3. Do you relate to Peter most when he bravely steps out of the boat or when he loses focus and begins to sink? Why?

GOD IS IN CHARGE
Day 6

As we become brave and take tentative steps—forward and perhaps backward our—hearts will begin to feel different. We sense things are changing and we begin to move toward brave faith. We may never arrive at our own understanding of brave faith because the process is evolving as we yearn to deepen our relationship with God.

I am discovering moments begin to feel brave like a step across the room to talk to someone I don't know or asking if I can pray for someone I just met. Each step is leading me to a heart change that God is slowly preparing me for in my walk. Eventually my steps will become strong and steady and I will see myself as God sees me—a brave woman!

Brave looks good on us when we start to experience a heart change. Brave is becoming and choosing God to work in us. Brave is pointing to God while keeping our eyes focused on His truths. Brave is knowing God is in charge.

Brave is allowing God to work in us, focusing our eyes on His truths and knowing He is in charge.

Verses for Reflection:

Hebrews 6:1
Psalm 37:23-24
Proverbs 4:11-13

Take Five:
(Five minutes to reflect, journal or sit and be with God)

1. How will you continue to stay focused on God when everyday life pulls you in a different direction?

2. In a world in which people like to be in control, how will you let go and let God lead your steps?

3. Write down three ways you will choose brave and allow God to work in you.

BRAVE NEEDS COMMUNITY
Day 7

A journey to brave faith cannot be done alone. Stepping into the unknown alone is not brave; because even though it will work temporarily, there is a perseverance needed, which requires others to walk with us. Brave needs community.

Annie Downs, in *Let's All Be Brave*, shares her story of moving to Nashville and knowing no one at all. She just knew she was supposed to be there. She eventually found a community of young adults that met on Sunday nights for dinner, each contributing whatever they had to put together for a meal. From the beginning of her "Stone Soup" community, she discovered they had become family. Not only was she being physically fed, but spiritually as well. It became *"an incubator for little seeds of courage"*.

I love these words from Annie. They provide a much needed perspective about being brave. I pray you find them life giving also.

No one is brave alone. Every superhero has someone they come home to; every Bible character has someone they depend on. Jesus had his disciples and his family. Batman had Robin. Paul had Barnabas. Ruth has Naomi. The Incredibles had each other; Superman had Lois Lane. Moses had Aaron, Hur, and Miriam. Noah had his family. So we see modeled, even in the Bible, the truth that the bravest among us do not stand alone.

Every superhero

needs someone to come home to

Annie Downs

Passage Through Grace

#bravefaith

Verses for Reflection:

Ruth 1:16-18
Exodus 4: 14-17
Hebrews 10: 24-25

Take Five:
(Five minutes to reflect, journal or sit and be with God)

1. Who are your people and how do they make you brave?

2. Choose either the verses from Ruth or Exodus above. Write out the importance of the relationships described in helping these pairs to become brave.

3. If you believe brave is not stepping into the unknown alone, can you call yourself brave? Why or why not?

A PLACE WHERE WE BELONG
Day 8

Brave needs community. We are made stronger when we are surrounded with people who love and support us. Community fills in the gaps of our weaknesses with the glue of love and acceptance. We are brave because we don't let our weaknesses consume us, but instead use them to our advantage by turning to God for guidance and grace.

Community fills in the places we are lacking and adds the bonus of building up and into us as we sometimes stumble and fall. Brave cannot persevere when we choose to do it alone. So choose community today to walk bravely forward to your next step.

I have found my brave journey to be similar in that when I began in earnest, it was with a small group of people from my church that all met together to begin this journey. Learning what my brave step was became clearer after hearing from this group and what brave looked like for them. We are never asked to take that first step toward brave alone.

Verses for Reflection:

Romans 15:7
John 13:20
John 13:34

Take Five:
(Five minutes to reflect, journal or sit and be with God)

1. Where is the one place you feel loved and accepted?

2. How do people in your community challenge you to be brave?

3. John 13:20 says, "whoever accepts anyone I send, accepts me". Knowing we have a need to belong, how will this help you to reach out in brave faith to others as you seek to grow closer to God?

BEING BRAVE RIGHT WHERE YOU ARE
Day 9

In August 2015, I was at a Five Minute Friday retreat near Nashville. Seventeen ladies gathered together to learn about the craft of writing, facing our fears of comparison and eventually how to walk bravely to face those fears. As I was leading a devotional on Sunday morning about being brave, new perspectives were shared as to what this looks like for some of the other women who were present.

The biggest "Aha" for me is that brave can look like staying right where you are and not taking that leap forward. God calls us in so many different ways and just because we are not saving the world doesn't mean we are not walking bravely right where God has us for this time in our lives.

This past year as I began a new normal as a retired teacher, I imagined that God was going to finally put me to the test of stepping out bravely for Him. Never once did I realize that it would look nothing like my made up dreams.

The year unfolded rather quietly and I fell into a rhythm that carried me through half of October. Life changed as my dad started experiencing some health problems and needed my care. What looked like a task to undertake became one of the bravest things I have ever done. Walking beside my dad as he struggled taught me lessons of bravery that I have never experienced before. Honoring him and leaning into his gentle strength was the greatest gift I received from my dad.

I needed to be present for my dad in a way that would not have been possible If I was still working full time. God knows our stories and what we need just when we need it. He knew that brave faith during this time was not trying to fulfill all of my dreams, but instead it was staying put right beside my dad.

Verses for Reflection:

James 5:7
Psalm 130:5
Matthew 11:28

Take Five:
(Five minutes to reflect, journal or sit and be with God)

1. Where do you find the brave in your season of waiting?

2. God asks us to come to Him when we are weary and
He will give us rest. Take a few minutes and journal
how God will always provide what we need.

3. If you are in a season of waiting or you recall a time
when you were, take time to write down what you
learned in the process.

BRAVE IN THE STAYING
Day 10

My dear friend, Holly Barrett, understands what living in a season of waiting is all about. She describes it as "brave in the staying". Her perspective alone is brave, but she takes it a step further by living out her brave faith. She teaches us how to accept where we are right now in our lives because that is the place God has called us to be.

Holly shares:

"There have been several times in my life when others called me brave. Leaving an abusive marriage is certainly not for the faint of heart. Single-parenting isn't either. We often think of brave as something that we do...or pursue...or achieve. But I recently learned that being brave may just be none of those things.

Sometimes brave is staying right where you are, even though it's not where you want to be. But for whatever His purposes are, God has called you to be still. That's exactly where He has me right now. In a place not of my choosing. In a place exactly opposite of where I'd love to be. To be honest, I've fought it hard. And all that has accomplished is to prolong my own despair.

Now that God is calling me to be brave in the staying, I'm trying to lean into the uncomfortable. I want to listen for what He had in mind when He brought me here. And to discover contentment in the place He chose for this season.

I want to be brave."

Verses for Reflection:

Psalm 17:4-5 MSG
Ecclesiastes 3:12-13
Psalm 119:82

Take Five:
(Five minutes to reflect, journal or sit and be with God)

1. If you have always believed brave is pursuing or achieving something, how does it make you feel to know that sometimes brave is staying right where you are?

2. Have you ever been in a season where you felt stuck? Did you feel brave? Why or why not?

3. Read Psalm 17:4-5 MSG. How do these words spur you on to be brave in the staying?

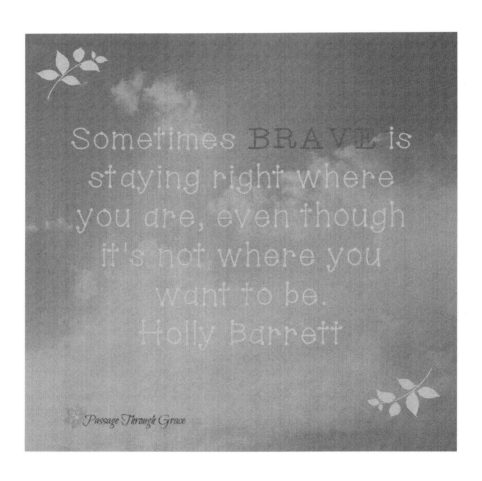

Sometimes BRAVE is staying right where you are, even though it's not where you want to be.
Holly Barrett

Passage Through Grace

NOT MY WILL, BUT YOURS
Day 11

How do we accept that God knows best when we are yearning for something different?

Being brave is a journey of walking forward or staying in a holding pattern. We learn to accept brave right where we are because it is God's will. Brave faith does not look like leaping over tall buildings every time we step foot out the front door.

So how do we bravely pray the words from Luke 22 below? How do we let God's will for our lives become our will of acceptance and love?

Our passage to brave faith is never without twists and turns. A step forward could end up in five steps backwards. Only God can see us through to the end— an end that He has already planned for us. Our goal is to agree to step out with God on this journey and when we say "yes", we accept God's will.

Father, if you are willing, take this cup from me; yet not my will, but yours be done. Luke 22:42

My brave journey placed me in a season of waiting in the last year. My focus has been on being still and allowing God to prepare my heart for what is next. In the staying still, I opened my heart to God's word and let His truth fill me. My time of waiting has not been one of feeling stuck, but one of preparation and letting God guide me toward my future.

Verses for Reflection:

Luke 22:42
Mark 11:22-24
Nehemiah 1

Take Five:
(Five minutes to reflect, journal or sit and be with God)

1. Pray the words of Luke 22 today. Let God fill you with faith as you say "yes" to Him.

2. How do you accept the truth God knows best even as you yearn for something different?

3. Take a few minutes and read Nehemiah 1. Write in your journal how Nehemiah displays his own brave faith as he learns about the plight of his people.

WHEN BRAVE LOOKS LIKE STAYING PUT
Day 12

Our lives don't look anything like we plan at times and we are frustrated over not being able to control all the details. But what if that is exactly what God is trying to teach us? What if the lesson is learning we are not in charge, but instead we are being asked to release the details to God?

My friend LeeAnn Taylor is asking those very questions. She is learning to release the details of the path her life is taking by changing her perspective about where God is currently calling her to be. Instead of feeling stifled by ordinary life, LeeAnn is embracing the here and now. Her words are a testimony to what brave faith looks like.

"For me, being brave in this season looks like staying put. In the middle of the day-to-day routine of working outside the home, parenting, loving my husband, managing my home, serving others, navigating financial pressures and more, the anxiety feels crushing some days.

Sometimes in the midst of the whirlwind, in the quiet moments of my daily commute, my mind wanders. I dream of all the possibilities for pursuing my passions, those things that stir my heart and make me come alive with excitement and purpose. But then I remember the weight of my current responsibilities and the discouragement creeps in.

I heard someone say recently that during the times we feel buried, maybe instead we're actually being planted.

There it is, the change in perspective. What if I stopped viewing my current situation as limiting and started casting off that feeling of being buried under all the responsibilities? What if instead I recognized this season as one of being brave as I stay put? God is planting me and growing me in faith so I can begin to grasp the depth and breadth of His love for me!"

I pray that out of his glorious riches he may strengthen you with power through his Spirit in your inner being, so that Christ may dwell in your hearts through faith. And I pray that you, being rooted and established in love, may have power, together with all the Lord's holy people, to grasp how wide and long and high and deep is the love of Christ, and to know this love that surpasses knowledge—that you may be filled to the measure of all the fullness of God. Ephesians 3:16-19

Verses for Reflection:

Ephesians 3:16-19
2 Corinthians 8:10-12
Philippians 1:3-6

Take Five:
(Five minutes to reflect, journal or sit and be with God)

1. How can you change your perspective if brave looks like staying put?

2. LeeAnn shares that during times we feel buried, maybe we're actually being planted. How do these words challenge you today?

3. Choose one of the Scripture passages and journal the blessings God promises in light of your circumstances.

BLOOM WHERE YOU ARE PLANTED
Day 13

When I was growing up, summertime looked like swimming lessons, lots of time playing outside with my brothers and the neighborhood kids and gardening. For many summers, my dad and I worked on a small vegetable garden. Tomato plants and green peppers were staples each year while other vegetables rotated in and out.

Working in a garden, side by side with my dad, provided many lessons. But it is the soul work that sticks with me to this day.

Gardening looks a lot like the soul work God does in and through us. The roots of the plants are like the anchors God throws out to save us and keep us steady. The fruits of the plants are the gifts God blesses us with and the ones we choose to use to honor Him. The branches represent the community of people who nurture, nourish and support us just as God does for His children. The soul work of God is ongoing, creates a better future and teaches us how to live in love as His child. In order for a garden to produce a bountiful harvest, the work to maintain it is ongoing and persistent.

If we are seeking to bloom where we are planted and allow God to make us brave where we are, we need to embrace these lessons:

Provide a space for the work that is needed.

Work hard to persevere even when we cannot see the fruits of our labor.

Allow God to prune and nourish us with His Word.

Feed yourself God's truth to establish a strong root system.

Embrace community and let them nurture and build into you.

God will provide the deep and lasting soul work and increase your courage as you pursue Him.

Verses for Reflection:

Psalm 37:5
Isaiah 26:4
Matthew 6:33-34

Take Five:
(Five minutes to reflect, journal or sit and be with God)

1. Look at the five lessons above. Choose one that you can start working on today.

2. The words in Matthew 6 challenge us not to worry about tomorrow because tomorrow will take care of itself. In the process of letting go of fear and anxiety, how do these words comfort you?

3. I use the analogy of a garden to describe soul work. What is another analogy you can wrap your head around to aid you in this journey to brave faith?

WHEN BRAVE IS THE LIFE YOU NEVER IMAGINED
Day 14

As we continue to look at being brave right where we are we discover it is not the big step that is headline-worthy or the kind of brave that has you shaking in your boots. This kind of brave looks ordinary to most and for others you would question if it fits into the same category as "leaping from tall buildings". But to those living it out, this brave is extraordinary. When God calls us to be brave at home, He knows He is calling us to put our dreams on hold to fulfill His will. It's when brave is the life you never imagined!

My friend, Jen Daugherty, describes the brave journey that took her away from home only to bring it full circle to where she started.

"I didn't want to move back to my hometown. Ever. It's not that I didn't enjoy growing up there, but rather that I saw no future there. I equated moving back with failure, because nobody ever wanted to move there. Everyone wanted to get out.

And so I graduated from college and moved abroad, looking forward to visiting home, but never living there again. Now, 4 years after leaving, I've found myself living back in my hometown, holding a permanent job, and planting deep roots. Almost unwillingly at first, but now eagerly looking forward to investing in a community I've come to love. Staying was difficult. It was most certainly unwanted. And it took a whole lot of brave to choose to stay.

Sometimes the bravest thing we can do is stay where we are. Some people live a life of planes, suitcases, and new languages, and that is brave. But some people live a life of community meetings, walking, school buses, and movies in the park. Living well where you are takes a lot of bravery, especially when it was never the life you imagined. Growing roots and investing in those around you takes courage. But the power of being brave right where you are? It's incalculable."

Verses for Reflection:

Ezekiel 17:5-7
Colossians 2:6-7
Proverbs 27:8

Take Five:
(Five minutes to reflect, journal or sit and be with God)

1. Colossians 2:6 calls us to continue to live our lives in Christ. Journal what this looks like for you.

2. Jen's journey took her abroad only to return back home at the end of four years. How is returning home a braver step than living abroad for four years?

3. When you are called to remain brave in the waiting, do you still allow yourself time to dream?

STAYING TRUE TO OUR CALLING
Day 15

God blesses each of us with brave faith even when brave is the very last thing we are feeling. In the staying, we become brave because God blesses each step of our journey.

In our lives, we can feel we are going nowhere fast. Our lives are consumed by our "to do" list and anything beyond the list does not seem to exist. God assures us that just because we are not leaping forward into adventure with Him, we are doing important work. *Will we accept the call to brave faith in the days of waiting and living our ordinary? Will we stay the course by staying true to our calling and who God has chosen us to be today, tomorrow and for always?*

Walking brave is not always a bigger and better step than what others are doing around us. Staying small in our own neighborhoods can impact our lives and those around us if we follow God's lead. Remembering who we are as God's child allows God to complete the work He has started in us.

Knowing that staying still in this moment does not mean we are stuck, is a beautiful reminder to allow God to grow our brave faith right where we are. Holding onto His promises and truth in all will bring us closer to Him and that, my friends, is brave faith being lived out for others to see.

Verses for Reflection:

1 Corinthians 1:26-31
2 Peter 1:10-11

Take Five:
(Five minutes to reflect, journal or sit and be with God)

1. Will you stay the course by staying true to your calling and who God has chosen you to be?

2. Walking in brave faith does not always mean bigger and better than what others are doing around you. Name three things you have done today that are brave.

WHEN BRAVE IS OUR KINGDOM WORK
Day 16

No matter where we are or what we are called to, we are brave when we choose God's work over our agenda. His kingdom is everywhere and we can make a difference right where we are.

Today we hear from my friend, Marcy Hanson, as she shares one more brave look at an ordinary life that in reality is oh so extraordinary. Her kingdom work is in her own city and neighborhood. Read her beautiful words to hear her story of brave faith.

"Brave seems to be the word of the day… month…year. It's been almost a catch-phrase, like 2015 is all about the brave and how you can show your courage. But I'm finding that brave looks a lot more like laying down than standing up. It feels a lot more like staying still than running towards battle. Right now, brave looks like driving home and having the courage to stay.

It's not the kind of brave I want to be. I want to jump. I want to feel the adrenaline rush of a new adventure. I want to feel like I'm living a purpose, not just with purpose. But right now that's not the brave

I'm called to.

I don't live in a war-torn country, but I live with war-torn hearts. With souls that have been broken down and are hurting. And when they hurt, they fight back and lash out at perceived threats. Even when that perception is wrong. For now, my brave is trying to mend those hearts. It is pulling close and holding tight even when others are pushing away. For me, brave looks a whole lot like everyday, and I'm learning to be okay with that. Because no matter what type of brave you're called to, it's all Kingdom work, and really, that's all that matters."

Verses for Reflection:

Matthew 6:33-34
Romans 14:17-18
1 Thessalonians 2:11-12

Take Five:
(Five minutes to reflect, journal or sit and be with God)

1. Marcy believes that no matter what your brave looks like, it is all kingdom work. What does this look like in your life?

2. Is brave faith living with purpose? Spend a few minutes journaling your answer.

3. Read Matthew 6:33-34. Journal your reflections in light of embracing your brave faith as kingdom work.

Because no matter what type of brave you're called to, it's all Kingdom work, and really, that's all that matters.
Marcy Hanson

#bravefaith

GIVING THANKS FOR BRAVE WHERE WE ARE
Day 17

Is it possible to not only be brave right where we are at this time in our lives, but also give thanks for the gift of present circumstances? Can we enjoy our here and now as the plan God has placed in our lives?

Today, as we continue to look at brave faith, let's rejoice that God has us in this place, at this time for our good and His. May we take the ordinary routines of our lives and complete them in joy and thanksgiving. We were made to be God's and as His children we are asked to build His kingdom in our present and future.

Ann Voskamp challenges us to count our blessings in the ordinary moments of our lives. In her book, *One Thousand Gifts*, she shares her personal life journey that brought her to the place of turning to God. In those vulnerable moments she found renewed joy in counting each gift that God graced her with on any given day. This simple act changed the trajectory of her life.

She names the bravery in focusing on all things good and giving thanks for it. This quote highlights

Ann's perspective of brave faith.

The brave who focus on all things good and all things beautiful and all things true, even in the small, who give thanks for it and discover joy even in the here and now, they are the change agents who bring fullest Light to all the world.
Ann Voskamp

Passage Through Grace

#bravefaith

Verses for Reflection:

Matthew 6:33-34
Ephesians 1:3-4
Matthew 5:3-12

Take Five:
(Five minutes to reflect, journal or sit and be with God)

1. Spend a few minutes giving thanks for the gift of being exactly where God planned for you to be.

2. Is it not only possible to be brave in the waiting but also give thanks for your circumstances?

3. Beginning today, count the blessings in your everyday ordinary and watch your joy multiply.

DO NOT BE AFRAID
Day 18

Our brave journey continues whether we are ready or not. Many times it's not the way we imagine it would unfold or in the timing that fits our plans, but the bottom line is it's always God's way, not ours. Brave faith is a reliance on God for His way and timing to be revealed. It is knowing that even in the waiting, the big "noes" or the sudden change in direction, that "God's got this." He is holding us close and desires for our heart to beat in rhythm and harmony with His.

Brave faith is releasing everything to God. It is turning our fear to God and putting on the armor of "do not be afraid for I am your God". There is not one thread of our being that is really ours. It belongs to God. Fear may block our vision, our path and our dreams, but God sees the whole tapestry of our lives. That is all we need.

The journey to brave faith requires knowing God and His truths. It is immersing ourselves in His Word and making it part of the fabric of our being. It is learning scripture and storing it in our hearts.

Today our journey takes us to God's Word and the healing strength we find within. Spend time praying and reflecting on the verses for reflection today.

Verses for Reflection:

Isaiah 41:10 NLT
Psalm 27:14
Isaiah 41:6
Hebrews 4:16 NLT

Take Five:
(Five minutes to reflect, journal or sit and be with God)

1. Journal about your time reflecting on the verses above.

2. Write down your favorite "go-to" verses when you are seeking confidence in God's truth.

3. How will you take a step toward brave faith by releasing everything to God?

SAYING YES WHEN YOU WANT TO SAY NO
Day 19

One of the first words a baby learns is the word "No". It flies out of his/her mouth one day and you look up in sheer joy because your child is talking. Your happiness over your child talking quickly becomes frustration when every other word uttered is "No". The cute factor changes into determination as you teach your child other vocabulary options, which most probably will include the word "Yes".

As an adult I am quick to say "yes" to many things in my life as my people-pleasing personality rules my mind and decisions quite often. I realize that a balance is needed between my yeses and noes to temper my life and the pendulum that leans heavily to the people-pleasing side. But life is not always controlled by us. In fact life is not ours to control at all.

I know how life can change in the blink of an eye and it has nothing to do with how many times I have already said "yes". Four years ago, I experienced a major life change with my job and my only choice was to say "yes" when my heart was screaming "no". Losing a job at the end of your career and then being given one option to stay in your field results in disbelief and upheaval. I pulled through only because the grace of God is bigger.

As I remember that day vividly and how things unfolded, I know now this was one of the bravest things I experienced. *Why brave, you ask?* I soon realized the only way I could successfully move forward into this other job was to hang onto God as tight as I could. It was messy, ugly and a huge blow to my ego. **But God**... He rescues us when we come to Him in humility and believe that He is the only way back to strength, faith and confidence. When we accept His grace as the gift that it was always meant to be and allow it to wash over us as a sweet balm of healing, we learn we are accepted and loved deeply by our Father.

Saying yes when you want to say no with your whole being is a lesson in faith. It is releasing your ego to God so He may bring healing in the midst of pain and struggle. It is wearing the armor of brave faith to walk humbly with God as He leads you to where He knew you needed to be all along.

Verses for Reflection:

Jeremiah 29:11
2 Corinthians 1:17-20
Job 22:21

Take Five:
(Five minutes to reflect, journal or sit and be with God)

1. If you are a person who is quick to say "yes", recall a time when God intervened with His own answer. What did that time look like?

2. Life can change in the blink of an eye. Reflect on any experience you had with this and how God guided you to embrace brave faith in the middle of the changes.

3. Spend time reading the verses above and invite God to join you in your quiet time as you begin to understand the truth that God's "yes" is always the best.

LET GOD TRANSFORM OUR NO INTO HIS YES
Day 20

I can remember times in my life when an adamant "no" came flying out of my mouth. I would rather kick and scream than give up my "no" because in that moment I felt justified that I was right. I am a grown adult and pushing back in the form of a mini tantrum is not pretty, but standing strong in my position seems the only way to go at times. **What can we possibly believe is worth that much of a fight?**

Life experience adds restraint and understanding to situations that I did not always have when I was younger. I learned that getting my way at any expense is not the choice God wishes for me to choose. I found I can back off and let go when I turn to God to advise me in difficult times.

We find beauty when we are handed a "no" answer because God's "yes" is exactly what we needed. We allow God's truth to permeate our choices and turn our adamant "no" into His beautiful "yes".

God's grace is transforming and accepting this gift allows us to pause and carefully choose what God desires rather than what we stubbornly are fighting for.

We do not become brave in our faith by overriding God's decisions. We grab brave faith when our heart is in sync with God's desires for our journey. Today we can let God transform our no into His yes because we choose brave faith and God's truth as our answer.

With grace and bravery, let's walk away from our stubborn "noes" to God's beautiful "yeses".

We allow God's truth to permeate our choices so our adamant "no" becomes His beautiful "yes" for our lives.

Verses for Reflection:

Proverbs 16:3
Proverbs 19:21
Psalm 33:11

Take Five:
(Five minutes to reflect, journal or sit and be with God)

1. Recall a time when letting go of your answer or point of view left you kicking and screaming. Spend a few minutes releasing this to God.

2. How would brave faith aid you in letting God's truth permeate your choices?

3. Allow God's grace to wash over any decisions made out of ego rather than acceptance of God's answer. Journal your reflections.

Wear the ARMOR of brave faith and let God lead you home.

Passage Through Grace

#bravefaith

SAYING YES CHANGES EVERYTHING
Day 21

One brave "yes" leads to more "yeses" that can then lead to bigger brave moments and brave faith. Agreeing to step out of our comfort zone one time is a signal to God that we are ready for more. God knows when it is time to call us to more and it does not require that we have everything already figured out.

In my own life, brave is part of my life's journey, even though for many years I would not call it brave. In 2015, I joined members of my church for a brave journey that asked us to speak out loud what brave step God was calling us to take. I went into the six weeks apprehensive and came out on the other side bold in my decision. I said "yes" to going on a mission trip to Nicaragua that took place a year later. God honored my "yes" and saw it through every step of the way. As the plane touched down in Nicaragua, tears flowed as the realization hit me. God brought me to the place I said "yes" to visiting and everything changed.

Annie Downs talks brave faith throughout her book, *Let's All Be Brave*. Every word tells her story and her journey to brave, but when we dig into what this can look like for us, we find out that her stories could very well center around us as the main character.

These words from Annie have been stirring in my heart ever since I read her book.

> Saying yes changes everything. Walking through the door, agreeing in the moment. Sometimes it is just what is needed to show you the next big yes... We have to say yes. Even when it's scary or costly or unknown. We don't screw up by saying yes to the wrong things; we screw up by letting all the floats in the parade pass us by and never jumping on one of them for a ride to the end.

God's "yes" for our lives should align with our choices. When we say "yes", we are choosing God's plan over our agenda. The times when we crave everything but a "yes", are the times God calls us to step out boldly for Him. Saying yes changes everything and leads us closer to brave faith.

Verses for Reflection:

Leviticus 20:8
Deuteronomy 28:1
Psalm 23:6

Take Five:
(Five minutes to reflect, journal or sit and be with God)

1. Journal about a time you said "yes" to God. Describe what that looked like.

2. God honors our "yeses" and provides goodness all the days of our lives. Take some time in thanksgiving and prayer for these blessings in your life.

3. A journey to brave faith requires multiple "yeses" in order to move from fear to God. Write down your next "yes" and share it with a friend.

Ordinary Brave
Day 22

Have you considered how brave you already are? Did you think it was possible that you are brave each time you make a decision in your everyday, ordinary life?

When we choose God in our everyday decision making, we are asking for His direction. This is such an important step on our journey to brave faith. We are acknowledging that we are made stronger and more able with His help. Taking our uncertainties, struggles, routines, and ordinary to God and releasing it makes us brave. We take a huge step forward through this release and it empowers us to be brave.

Emily P. Freeman describes ordinary moments as Tuesday moments in her book, *Simply Tuesday*. It is remembering that Jesus shows up in the daily ordinary of washing dishes, carpooling, making dinner or helping your kids with their homework. Tuesday is the day of the week that is completely ordinary by default. All the other days are marked by being first, in the middle or the weekend.

When we let go of ourselves and release our

mundane to God, let's stop and consider the brave in these moments. Let's think like Emily and instead of dismissing them as routines, embrace them as *"unlikely portals into the kingdom of God where the goal isn't to set them aside but to recognize Christ with us in the midst of them."*

Verses for Reflection:

Colossians 3:17
Galatians 6:9-10
1 Corinthians 13

Take Five:
(Five minutes to reflect, journal or sit and be with God)

1. Is it possible to feel brave faith in the routines of life?

2. Journal where Christ shows up in your ordinary life. Describe how these routines are brave.

3. Read 1 Corinthians 13. How would living your life as described in this chapter help you to embrace brave faith?

BRAVE FAITH
Day 23

When the hardest "yes" is the answer you know you must give even though you are screaming "no" on the inside...

When a decision causes trepidation in your heart, but ultimately will provide comfort for your soul ...

When saying "yes" is the bravest thing you will do...

then you know you have turned the corner to brave faith. You are one step closer to the brave that God knew you always had in you. The "yes" you answer is the one God has craved to hear since you were born.

This scenario played out not too long ago in my own life. A community I had been invited to join and spend time with was the very one that I now needed to say "no" to hanging with. A time to share encouragement every other weekend with other beautiful writers needed to happen in a different setting. God was closing the door on this weekend community in respect to what He knew I needed.

Brave happens in every decision you make. You will find it in your yeses and noes. Brave is in you as you navigate your daily routines and seek to understand the challenges in front of you. Brave happens everyday and this journey we are on together to brave faith is an example that even though you might not consider yourself "brave", God and those around you do! **Do you feel a difference since the first time you entered this walk with me?** I know I do!

> *This is what the Lord says—your Redeemer, the Holy One of Israel: "I am the Lord your God, who teaches you what is good for you and leads you along the paths you should follow."* Isaiah 48:17

When we are asked to do the hard things and our reaction is to fight it every step of the way, we know God is leading us to a new brave. He is equipping us for the journey and He is making ready the path we need to follow.

Letting God take charge always leads us to our destination, which is life in and for Him. Brave faith is how we get there.

Verses for Reflection:

2 Corinthians 5:7
Isaiah 48:17
1 Corinthians 16:13

Take Five:
(Five minutes to reflect, journal or sit and be with God)

1. How will you embrace brave faith today?

2. We read in Isaiah 48 that God teaches us what is good and leads us along the path we should go. How does this truth help you when you feel uncertain along the way?

3. What is your gut reaction when you are asked to do something hard? How will knowing God equips you for the journey make it easier?

Brave faith is when we allow God to lead us to our destination.

TRIUMPH OVER FEAR
Day 24

Do you remember as a child when someone dared you to do something in front of the other neighborhood kids? You wanted to save face in front of your friends, but your insides were quivering. Fear is a common reaction to many dares we are asked to conquer in our lives. Fear also creates a wall between us and that next step.

Many of us would argue that fear is the factor keeping us from brave. If our fears were kept at bay, we would have no difficulty ever being brave. Enter ME... I am by nature afraid of many things. Just telling me I can keep my fears in check, will not persuade me that I can be brave. I need something or someone to help me triumph over fear. It's more than an assurance that I can overcome. **What does this look like for you?**

God speaks to us over and over throughout the Bible. He repeats "do not be afraid" as a badge of comfort and means to overcome all we face in our daily challenges. We find this badge of truth beginning in the Book of Genesis. God speaks to Abram and says...

After this, the word of the Lord came to Abram in a vision: "Do not be afraid, Abram. I am your shield, your very great reward. Genesis 15:1

But God does not stop there and provides the armor of courage in Deuteronomy. He says...

Be strong and courageous. Do not be afraid or terrified because of them, for the Lord your God goes with you; he will never leave you nor forsake you. Deuteronomy 31:6

As we move into the New Testament, we are reassured that our fear will give way to peace as we continue to lean into God with our whole being. John's words teach us that our troubled hearts will be replaced with a peace that can only come from God.

Peace I leave with you; my peace I give you. I do not give to you as the world gives. Do not let your hearts be troubled and do not be afraid. John 14:27

When we read the words below from Nelson Mandela, we know that triumph over fear is possible because God will equip us with the armor of brave faith, when we choose to wear it with the belief that He conquers all fear.

I learned that courage was not the absence of fear, but the triumph over it. The brave man is not he who does not feel afraid, but he who conquers that fear. Nelson Mandela

May we embrace brave faith and wear it proudly as our badge of courage today.

Verses for Reflection:

John 14:27
Genesis 15:11
Joshua 1:9

Take Five:
(Five minutes to reflect, journal or sit and be with God)

1. Nelson Mandela challenges us with his words about courage. Read the quote and reflect on how you conquer fear in your own life.

2. How will you wear the armor of brave faith today?

3. If fear is your "go-to" reaction, when asked to do something hard, spend time today asking God to release you from the fear.

BLINDLY BRAVE
Day 25

Being blindly brave sounds like an oxymoron. How can you step out confidently if you cannot see where you are going?

The beauty is that God calls us to step out all the time into the unknown because He is teaching us what brave faith looks like.

The journey I am currently on is one that is preparing my heart to step out bravely for God. But as I desire to be bold for God, I am seeking, but not finding. I am left with many questions, but no answers.

Brave requires perseverance in the face of questions and in the times of stillness, to allow the answers to find us. Stepping out for God is what we are called to do even when it looks like we do not know where we are going. It means we are letting God do His brave work in us as preparation for the bold steps that will surely come.

In my time of retirement, I am looking ahead to

follow God's lead into my what's next. The horizon is fuzzy in the distance as I open my heart to saying "yes" but God will make that clear in His time. All I can do is let the inside work continue as God readies me for this next step. I hold onto His truth and know that the unknown is replaced by the known when we keep our faith in sync with God.

I have no quick fixes to offer when we are faced with choosing to be brave. There are no neat and tidy steps to follow when our next steps are unknown. My best answer is to keep our hearts open to adopting bold answers from God. Stay ready in the preparation and in the stillness before God's call becomes clear. Accept God's call when it comes and say "yes" to what's next. Continue to have a vision for the future-dream a little and take steps forward with the assurance that God will open doors or close them according to His plan. In the times of waiting and uncertainty, wait expectantly for all God will bring in this journey to brave.

Remember, *brave is looking through the glass even when the view is unclear.* It is embracing hope for what is to come and trusting that God always knows best. It is taking baby steps forward through the unknown while trusting God every step of the way.

Verses for Reflection:

1 Thessalonians 2:11-12
Mark 1:16-17
1 Thessalonians 5:23-24

Take Five:
(Five minutes to reflect, journal or sit and be with God)

1. How do you step out confidently if you cannot see where you are going?

2. In Mark 1, Jesus calls Simon and his brother Andrew to be his first disciples. Jesus also calls us to step forward and follow Him. Reflect on what this calling looks like in your own life.

3. Brave requires perseverance. How will you embrace this truth today?

EMBRACE GOD
Day 26

Throughout this brave journey, the one constant has always been God. When we choose Him to walk with us as well as turn to Him in fear and uncertainty, we are choosing brave over everything else. It sounds simple, but we know it is anything but simple!

The world is big and comes at us from all sides in the workplace, our homes, through social media, those we come in contact with and the list goes on. Fear is real and can consume us without us really knowing it is happening. **How do we turn our backs on the fear that threatens to overwhelm us?**

The only answer I know is to embrace God in the midst of those uncertainties and fear and hold on to His truths and promises. I wrote in an earlier post this year that brave is putting on the armor of God and walking forward in courage to what He calls you to do in your life. It is the outer strength that wraps the inner core of fear with a desire to step out and say "yes".

Those words have impacted me in my journey to brave faith. They are teaching me we are not meant to walk alone in facing our fears. **We are stronger** because we choose God.

There are five words that we can play on repeat as we look for brave and learn how to make it our own. I pause the messy and turn to this mantra when life needs to rewind back to God ... **"I can't, but He can!"** Five words that can make all the difference when you are frozen with fear or uncertain how to proceed. I am blessed that these words were first shared with me by my son. He has made "I can't, but He can" his mantra. It is his reminder, inspiration, encouragement and strength when brave is overshadowed by challenges and strength is getting beat up by weakness. When the light at the end of the tunnel is not even a pin prick or the mountain of life is too steep to climb, these five words beat a steady drum beat.

I want to leave you with some encouragement that we all can embrace as we journey to brave faith. It is taking on an "I can't, but He can" attitude as well as understanding what courage looks like. Praying for you all today as we learn together that the journey to brave is hard but oh so easy when we choose God to lead the way.

Courage is saying "yes" when the popular answer is "no". Courage is letting God take the lead as we follow in faith. Courage is embracing the Word of God as truth and soaking in the words that God gifted us with so many years ago. Courage is embracing the privilege of God walking beside us each and every day.

Verses for Reflection:

Isaiah 40:8
Matthew 4:4
1 John 2:14

Take Five:
(Five minutes to reflect, journal or sit and be with God)

1. How do you turn your back on the fear that threatens to overwhelm you?

2. Allow "I can't, but He can" to become your breath prayer this week. Let the words become as steady and rhythmic as breathing in and out.

3. Write your own statement of courage.
Courage is ...

ONE MORE STEP
Day 27

I am finding that brave does not happen when you allow yourself to be stuck. But being still and staying stuck are not the same. Still is when you are inviting God to be present in your quiet so you may center your thoughts on Him. It is not freezing in fear or uncertainty so that moving forward becomes impossible. Staying stuck is a conscious choice that involves no movement in thought or action. **So which will you choose? Staying still to quiet your mind and fill it with God or staying stuck, which has you frozen in time?**

Today we are looking at taking one more step. In our stillness, the challenges and times of seeking what's next, we might question how to take that next step. How do we extend grace to ourselves and others? How do we move forward when we we can't see the way? What does one more step look like when the challenge is bigger than ourselves?

Rachel Wojo, in her book, *One More Step*, takes us through her life and the challenges she faced all the while teaching us how to take one more step. Rachel points us to God's word and truth to carry us forward. Every step she took as she faced her own challenges was a brave step toward God, who she knew would ultimately carry her through.

After reading Rachel's words on necessary grace, I connected how grace is needed in our journey to brave faith. Any journey is full of bumps, twists and unexpected turns. The path to brave faith is no different. Rachel writes, "grace is truly something each of us needs, especially when we feel like giving up". How often do we want to end a journey when it doesn't seem to be leading us where we want to go or when the way gets too hard? The grace of God was first present when Jesus came to earth in human form. God gives us grace because He loves us just as He loved His Son. God's biggest desire is to walk with us as we learn to bravely say "yes" and to gift us with His grace along the way.

Rachel wisely writes, "The situation we wish God would remove from our lives are often the lessons God uses to teach us to rely on Him." When we accept God's grace and admit we are weak, we are learning to be brave. I love how God teaches us not only through his stories, but in the words of others who cross our paths. Rachel's book, *One More Step*, has done that for me.

In our stillness of mind and body, let's embrace God's grace as a gift for ourselves when we are uncertain of that next step. Let's be kind to ourselves when brave looks like preparing our heart and mind for all God is going to do. Brave is not always a huge step or an obvious action that others immediately attribute to being brave. It is a gift of releasing all to God so brave can fill the spaces in our hearts we emptied for God.

Brave is a journey. It is baby steps toward choosing God while at the same time surrendering ourselves to His plans. It is looking forward even if we are in a waiting period. I will leave you with these words from Rachel...

Consistent movement in the present is what propels us toward the future.

Verses for Reflection:

Psalm 37:23
Proverbs 16:9
1 Peter 2:20-21

Take Five:
(Five minutes to reflect, journal or sit and be with God)

1. Spend time today visualizing brave and how you will take that first step.

2. How will you extend grace to yourself today when you do not know what your next step should be?

3. Rachel Wojo teaches us "consistent movement in the present is what propels us toward the future." Spend time letting her words soak in and become part of your brave journey.

Consistent movement in the present is what propels us toward the future.

#bravefaith

BRAVE IS A STEP, NOT THE WHOLE STAIRCASE
Day 28

Have you ever tried to go up a staircase straddling more than one step at a time? If you have longer legs, it probably worked out okay for you, but there is the possibility that as you were stretching your legs for that next step, you did not quite reach it and you were hanging on precariously. A staircase is meant to be climbed one step at a time. A journey of brave faith is meant to be conquered one step at a time. The journey anywhere happens one step at a time. We do not get from A to Z without following the path and taking the steps needed to get there.

Martin Luther King puts this into perspective with these words… "You don't have to see the whole staircase, just take the first step." In other words, we just need to take that step. God will be there to guide us the rest of the way.

God teaches us new lessons all the time. Since the beginning of this year, He has had me on this journey to brave. He first started working in me when our church began a series on brave. The key verse that has been a constant reminder for me during this time is from Matthew 14. I have read this passage over and over and have found these words about Peter and the disciples inspiring and motivating on this path to brave faith.

The passage begins with Jesus asking his disciples to get in the boat while He dismissed the crowd of five thousand that had gathered to hear Him. Peter and the disciples proceed to the boat and as they are leaving the shore, a storm begins to increase with intensity. The disciples, frightened and hanging on desperately in the midst of the storm, see a figure coming toward them across the water. Thinking it is a ghost, terror arises anew. Just as they are shouting that it is a ghost, another voice calls out.

> But immediately Jesus spoke to them, saying, "Take heart; it is I. Do not be afraid."
> And Peter answered him, "Lord, if it is you, command me to come to you on the water." **He said, "Come." So Peter got out of the boat and walked on the water and came to Jesus.** But when he saw the wind, he was afraid, and beginning to sink he cried out, "Lord, save me." Jesus immediately reached out his hand and took hold of him, saying to him, "O you of little faith, why did you doubt?" And when they got into the boat, the wind ceased. And those in the boat worshiped him, saying, "Truly you are the Son of God." Matthew 14:27-32

Jesus beckons for us to take that one step. I am a toe dipper and immediately pull my foot out of the water if it doesn't feel just right. Peter did not test the waters first and instead immediately stepped out of the boat when Jesus said, "Come". He faithfully followed and took that first step. I included the rest of the passage to show that doubt creeps in when our eyes lose sight of Jesus. Peter does lose focus and this causes him to sink. Jesus just asks us to take that first step and trust Him.

Verse 29 portrays faith. It displays heeding the voice of Jesus and taking that first step. It's words describe when brave is one step, not the whole staircase. This verse has been on repeat in my life. It shows up at church, at conferences, in devotionals and in words that others share with me. It is God calling me, as well as all of us, to take that first step. **Be brave and step out of the boat.**

Verses for Reflection:

Matthew 14:27-32- take time reading these verses today as part of your quiet time with God

Take Five:
(Five minutes to reflect, journal or sit and be with God)

1. Will you take the first step out of the boat like Peter did?

2. Knowing that God calls us to take one step at a time, what will you put into place to take that first step?

3. How will you keep your eyes focused on Jesus as you take your first step?

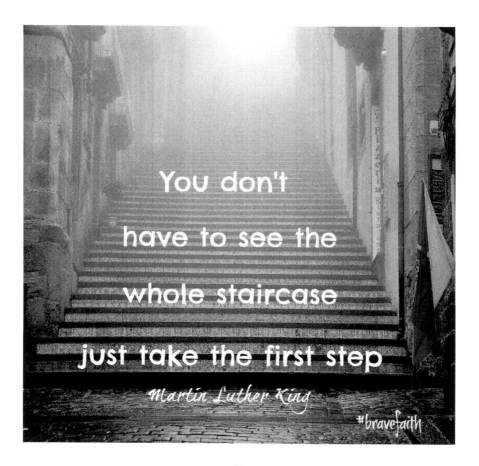

You don't have to see the whole staircase just take the first step

Martin Luther King

#bravefaith

BRAVE IN THE CALM
Day 29

Yesterday we looked at the story of Peter walking on the water after Jesus beckoned "Come". This one step is my inspiration for my faith journey. Peter's step out of the boat symbolizes a key component of brave faith that has spurred me on to writing this 31 day devotional. But last night, I began to imagine a scenario that looked different. What if....

The water that day was still, almost glassy in texture. The only ripple was caused by a pair of ducks out for their afternoon swim. The skies were blue. The sun was shining. Nothing indicated that one of the biggest bravest acts was going to take place. The calm that pervaded the surrounding area provided no warning of an event that would change the faith of one man.

Reflect on how brave can also happen on the calm days of our lives. Think about how brave does not require turmoil to be present in our lives. **How does this brave look different than the day Peter took his first step out of the boat to walk to Jesus?**

This question intertwines with all God is teaching me about brave and how we need brave no matter what our circumstances might be. Brave is stepping out of our comfort zones and reaching for God. When we consider this description of brave, I imagine we would agree that brave is in our every day ordinary as well as in the challenges that cross our paths. My comfort zone is small and stretching beyond it requires brave faith. God knows I am weak and I need Him on Sunday, Monday and every other day of the week. God reaches for me and as soon as I stretch out my arms in acceptance, I become brave.

Brave looks like the belief that God will do what He says He will do. It is allowing the gift of grace to fill us when everything else seems to be going wrong. It is a deep soul breath of renewal when exhaustion overwhelms and threatens to overcome. It is opening our eyes to the beauty present in our day. Finally, it is knowing God's love surpasses all other loves and is His gift to us daily.

Being brave in the calm is letting go of ourselves and our agenda each day. It is knowing that it is only through God we make it through the day. Brave is the release of ourselves while accepting God's plan. Brave is taking that first step out of the boat when Jesus calls, "Come". We can all be like Peter every time we take a brave step.

Verses for Reflection:

John 14:27
Luke 8:23-25
Isaiah 26:12

Take Five:
(Five minutes to reflect, journal or sit and be with God)

1. Are you brave in your daily life and routines?

2. What does brave currently look like in your life?

3. In Luke 8, as the disciples are terrified they are going to drown, Jesus calms the storm. Jesus is in the storm and is the calm influence we need. Jesus is the keeper of our brave faith at all times. Sit and allow yourself to embrace this truth in your quiet time.

WHAT IS YOUR CALL TO COURAGE?
Day 30

Today let's take a peek into our own hearts and dream big. Let's leap across the rocks marking the rugged path across the water. Be brave and say your dream out loud to a friend, family member or even your pet! What is your call to courage?

After reading the book, *Restless* by Jennie Allen, I discovered my gifts and how they meshed with the threads of my life. These threads when studied as a whole can reveal more about who you are and what areas you are gifted in as well as passionate about. Studying who I am by looking back as well as looking forward helped me to understand what has always been a passion of mine as well as how I developed or did not develop these passions over the years. My threads created a pattern that help me to understand how I can use my gifts currently to honor God. I still ask "what is my call to courage?" and spend time listening for answers from God. The blessing is that I know who I am in a deeper way and bravely seek God in the answers.

God calls us to courage. He plans beautiful things for our lives and then looks for a "yes" from us when He comes calling. God loves when we dream big and seek ways to build His kingdom. This is brave! He desires to align our dreams with His plan. Remember we are learning to stay still but not stuck. Listen well, heed God's voice, dream courageously and let the rest bloom where it is planted.

There is no right or wrong when it comes to being brave. Sometimes a "yes" is our brave answer, but other times saying "no" is the bravest thing we can do. Annie Downs writes about this in **Let's All Be Brave**. We are not going to get courage right all the time. The bottom line is to step out of the boat. Let God take care of the rest. Let these words from Annie Downs fill you today.

> I'm just not sure you are going to get it right every time – saying the right yes and the right no. I don't get it right all the time. But courage doesn't equal right; courage equals stepping out and trying. Be brave and say yes. But also be brave and say no… Say the thing that courage asks you to say, even if it's the word no.

Verses for Reflection:

Romans 11:29
Ephesians 4:1-2
Romans 12:5-7

Take Five:
(Five minutes to reflect, journal or sit and be with God)

1. What is your call to courage?

2. Annie Downs reminds us there is no right or wrong answers when it comes to brave. Write down Annie's words to keep somewhere as a daily reminder.

3. Spend time in prayer today listening for answers from God as you seek your call to courage.

YOU ARE BRAVER THAN YOU KNOW
Day 31

Over the course of this passage to brave faith, we covered many aspects of brave. As I began this journey of writing this devotional leading us to brave faith, I said the words "You are braver than you know" every morning to myself. I believe I am braver than I know. Do you believe you are braver than you know?

When fear is whispering into your ear, will you release it back to God?

When one more step is the biggest brave step you take, will you leap into the water and swim hard after Jesus?

When saying yes means choosing God over your agenda, can you stay strong and let Him lead the way?

When your whole being screams no, but God says yes, will you let Him transform your no into His beautiful yes?

When brave means staying right where you are and your dreams are pushed aside, will you stay true to who you are and who God is calling you to be in your life's journey?

You are braver than you know. Each day we make brave decisions in the daily routines, the challenges and every time we choose to step out of our comfort zones. Each brave decisions leads us one step closer to letting God take charge of our lives. It is trusting God's truths over our own. Brave happens everyday and strengthens us to be who God always knew we would be.

May these words from Ephesians strengthen you along your brave journey and remind you of God's endless love for you.

When I think of all this, I fall to my knees and pray to the Father, the Creator of everything in heaven and on earth. I pray that from his glorious, unlimited resources he will empower you with inner strength through his Spirit. Then Christ will make his home in your hearts as you trust in him. Your roots will grow down into God's love and keep you strong. And may you have the power to understand, as all God's people should, how wide, how long, how high, and how deep his love is. May you experience the love of Christ, though it is too great to understand fully. Then you will be made complete with all the fullness of life and power that comes from God. Ephesians 3:14-19 NLT

Verses for Reflection:

Ephesians 3:14-19
Psalm 119:105 NLT

Take Five:
(Five minutes to reflect, journal or sit and be with God)

1. Spend part of your time reflecting on the questions above.

2. Journal what your brave faith looks like now that you have reached the end of our 31 day journey.

3. The journey to brave faith is ongoing. It does not end today and most certainly not tomorrow. You are braver than you know! Thank God for the blessings He has shown you for the last 31 days.

ABOUT THE AUTHOR

Mary Geisen is a lover of deep, soul-filled conversations over coffee. She is the mom of two amazing, grown sons, lover of the beach and long walks outside. She is blessed to be a retired elementary teacher seeking God in the ordinary routines of life. Several years ago God called her to live courageously in her every day life. Her writing journey began as God's story for her life blossomed into written words. The power of God's words has inspired her walk toward healing, brave faith and drawing closer to God through the power of grace. You can find her at her writing home: www.passagethroughgrace.com

ENDNOTES

Annie Downs, *Let's All Be Brave Living Life with Everything You Have* (Grand Rapids, Michigan: Zondervan, 2014)

John Ortberg, *If You Want to Walk on Water You've Got to Get Out of the Boat* (Grand Rapids, Michigan: Zondervan, 2001)

Emily P. Freeman, *Simply Tuesday Small-Moment Living in a Fast-Moving World* (Grand Rapids, Michigan: Revell, 2015)

Ann Voskamp, *One Thousand Gifts Devotional* (Grand Rapids, Michigan: Zondervan, 2012)

Rachel Wojo, *One More Step Finding Strength When You Feel Like Giving Up* (Colorado Springs, Colorado: Waterbrook Press, 2015)

Jennie Allen, *Restless Because You Were Made for More* (Nashville, Tennessee: W Publishing, 2013)